The Spider and the Fly

POCKET
BOOKS

First published in Great Britain in 2002 by Simon & Schuster UK Ltd, Africa House, 64 - 78 Kingsway, London WC2B 6AH.

This edition published in 2003 by Pocket Books, an imprint of Simon & Schuster UK Ltd. • Originally published in the USA by Simon & Schuster Children's Books in 2002.

Text copyright © 1829 by Mary Howitt • Illustrations copyright © 2002 by Tony DiTerlizzi • All rights reserved, including the right of reproduction in whole or in part in any form.

Pocket Books and colophon are registered trademarks of Simon & Schuster. Book design by Tony DiTerlizzi and Greg Stadnyk • The text for this book is sent in Caslon Antique.

Printed in China 2 4 6 8 10 9 7 5 3 1 CIP catalogue record for this book is available from the British Library upon request. ISBN 0-743-47817-7

Based on the poem by **Mary Howitt**

With illustrations by **Tony DiTerlizzi**

"Will you walk into my parlour?" said the Spider to the Fly,

"'Tis the prettiest little parlour that ever you did spy;

The way into my parlour is up a winding stair,

And I have many curious things to show you when you are there."

"Oh no, no," said the little Fly, "to ask me is in vain,

For who goes up your winding stair can ne'er come down again."

"I'm sure you must be weary, dear, with soaring up so high;

Will you rest upon my little bed?" said the Spider to the Fly.

"There are pretty curtains drawn around; the sheets are fine and thin,

And if you like to rest awhile, I'll snugly tuck you in!"

"Oh no, no," said the little Fly, "for I've often heard it said,
They never, never wake again, who sleep upon your bed!"

Said the cunning Spider to the Fly, "Dear friend, what can I do,

To prove the warm affection I've always felt for you?

I have within my pantry, good store of all that's nice;

I'm sure you're very welcome – will you please to take a slice?"

"Oh no, no," said the little Fly, "kind sir, that cannot be,

I've heard what's in your pantry, and I do not wish to see!"

"Sweet creature!" said the Spider, "you're witty and you're wise,

How handsome are your gauzy wings, how brilliant are your eyes!

I have a little looking-glass upon my parlour shelf,

If you'd step in one moment, dear, you shall behold yourself."

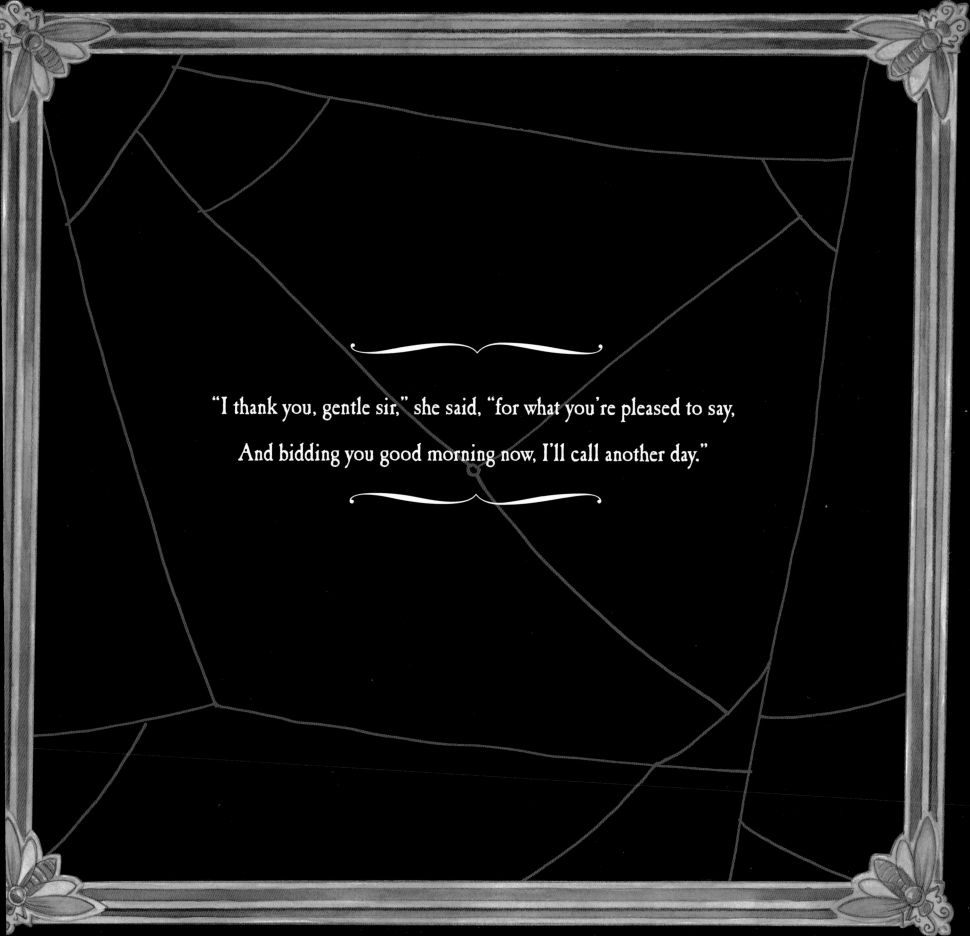

"I thank you, gentle sir," she said, "for what you're pleased to say,

And bidding you good morning now, I'll call another day."

The Spider turned him round about, and went into his den,

For well he knew the silly Fly would soon come back again:

So he wove a subtle web in a little corner sly,

And set his table ready, to dine upon the Fly.

Then he came out to his door again, and merrily did sing,

"Come hither, hither, pretty Fly, with the pearl and silver wing;

Your robes are green and purple – there's a crest upon your head;

Your eyes are like the diamond bright, but mine are dull as lead!"

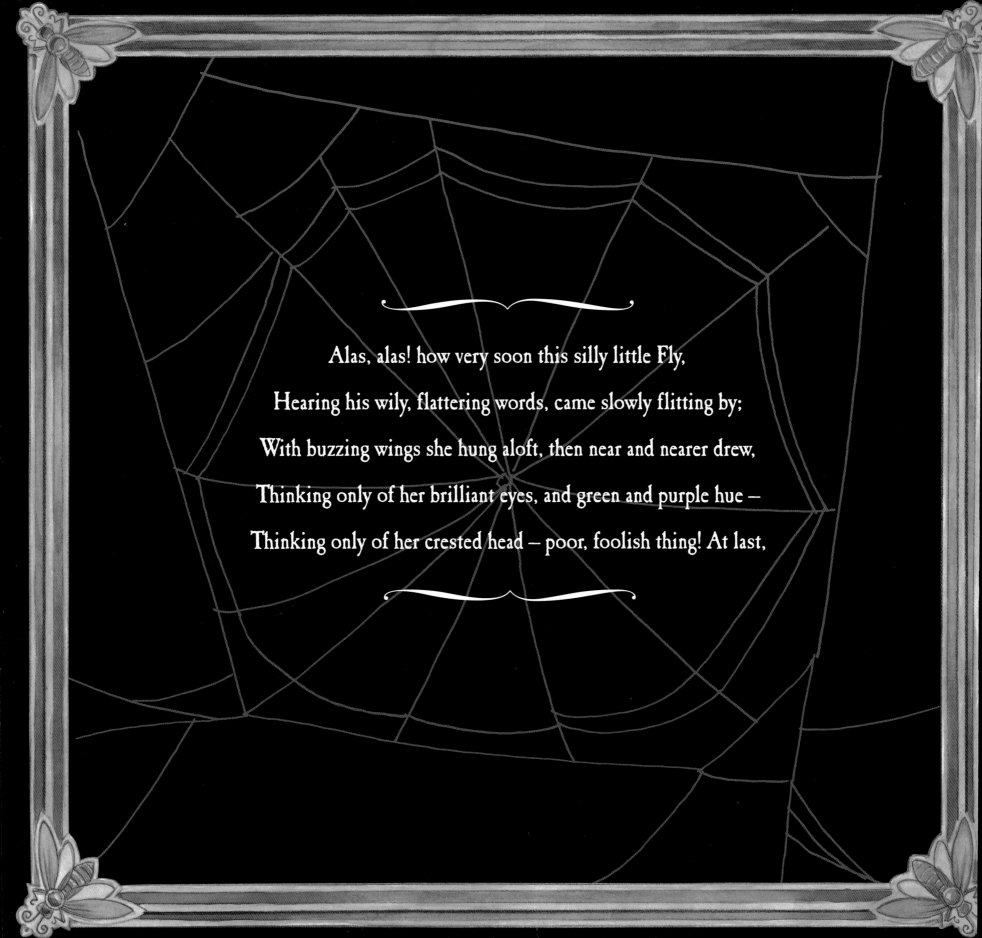

Alas, alas! how very soon this silly little Fly,

Hearing his wily, flattering words, came slowly flitting by;

With buzzing wings she hung aloft, then near and nearer drew,

Thinking only of her brilliant eyes, and green and purple hue –

Thinking only of her crested head – poor, foolish thing! At last,

Up jumped the cunning Spider,

and fiercely held her fast.

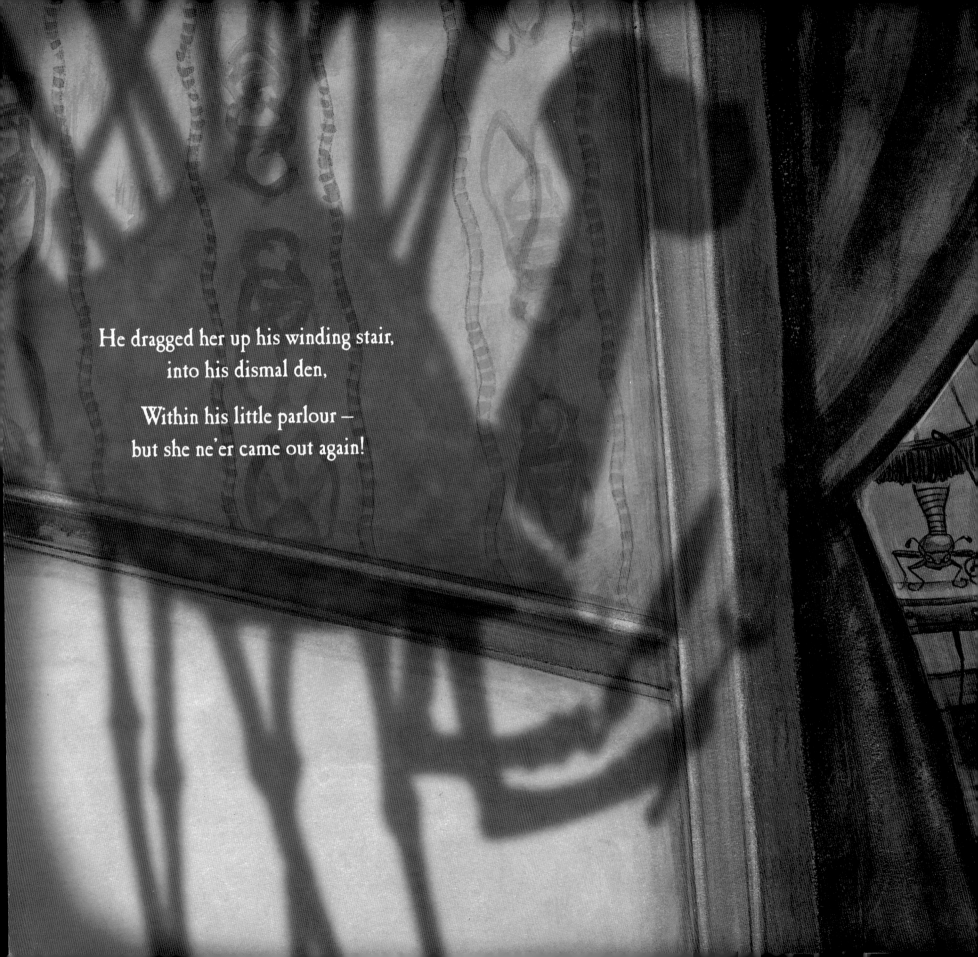

He dragged her up his winding stair,
  into his dismal den,

Within his little parlour —
  but she ne'er came out again!

And now, dear little children, who may this story read,

To idle, silly, flattering words I pray you ne'er give heed;

Unto an evil counsellor,
close heart and ear and eye,

And take a lesson from this tale,
of the Spider and the Fly.

R.I.P.

Dear Sweet Creatures,

No doubt you've finished our delicious tale and are surprised by this little tragedy, but then again, what did you expect from a story about a spider and a fly? Happily ever after? Spiders are trappers, for goodness sake! We've been doing it for generations, and we're quite good at it. Even your beloved Charlotte in E. B White's Charlotte's Web *admitted as much. But alas, the poor dear never capitalised on her fortune. Now if I were in her shoes, I would be eating bacon.*

With the wealth of knowledge about spiders and our crafty, carnivorous ways, you'd think my web would be empty, but not a day passes without a hapless bug or two stopping by. What's a spider to do? To be completely fair, my most recent dinner guest put up a commendable fight. But I am a talented and persistent hunter with many schemes up my sleeves. And you can see, I always get my bug.

So what does all this talk of spiders and traps have to do with you? Be warned, little dears, and know that spiders are not the only hunters and bugs are not the only victims. Take what has transpired within these pages to heart, or you might well find yourself trapped in some schemer's web.

Bon appetit,

Spider